This Book Belongs To :

Made in the USA
Monee, IL
27 February 2022

91926279R00069